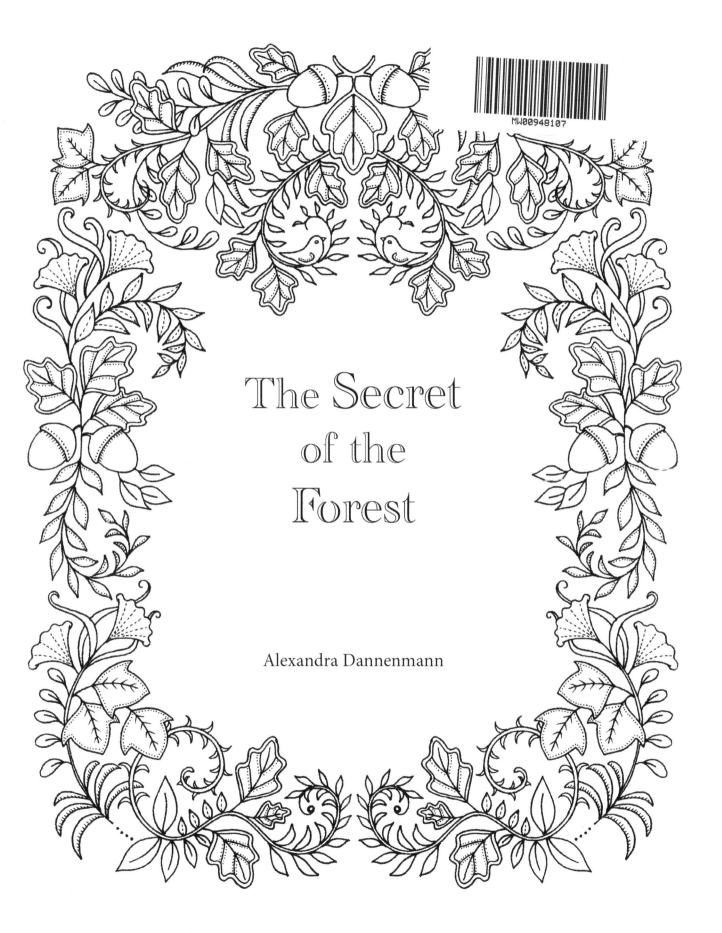

The Secret of the Forest

Alexandra Dannenmann

Find a bonus colouring sheet at
www.alexandra-dannenmann.de/free-download.

2nd edition: March 2016
Copyright © 2015 Alexandra Dannenmann
Text and illustrations: Alexandra Dannenmann – Stuttgart
Translation: S. T. Paterson
www.facebook.com/AlexandraDannenmann.Kinderbuch
www.alexandra-dannenmann.de
All rights reserved.
ISBN-13: 978-1518833953

This book belongs to:

The forest has concealed
its secret for many a long year:
a splendidly decorated little box
buried beneath leaves and mushrooms.

But a wily forest-dweller
has discovered the key
to the box - and with it
the precious jewels inside.

Look for the pieces of jewellery
hidden in some of the pictures,
and bring the forest to life
with vibrant colour.

Solutions

1 necklace

1 earring, 1 necklace

1 necklace

1 earring

1 necklace, 1 ring

1 necklace

1 necklace, 1 earring

1 necklace, 1 pendant,
1 ring

1 necklace

2 necklaces, 1 ring

1 ring

2 necklaces

1 necklace

1 necklace

2 necklaces

2 necklaces

2 necklaces

1 necklace

1 ring

1 earring, 1 necklace,
1 ring

1 necklace

3 necklaces, 1 earring,
1 ring, 1 key

More information and reading examples can be found on my homepage http://alexandra-dannenmann.de.

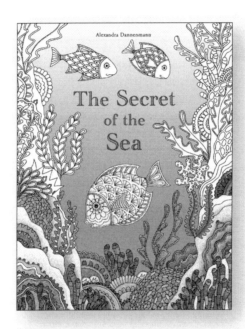

The Secret of the Sea
Search for hidden treasure from the sunken ship.

The sea has kept its secret hidden for many years: a sunken ship, loaded with the precious riches of a royal treasure chamber.

But storms and raging waves wrecked the ship and sent it plunging to the seabed.

Dive down into the depths of this enchanting water world, past exotic marine dwellers and rare water plants. Look for the treasures concealed in some of the pictures. And bring the underwater world to life with vibrant colour.

An enchanting colouring book that helps you forget everyday life and restores inner peace and balance. A book for discovery, for unwinding, and for dreaming.

With 45 richly detailed hand-drawn illustrations waiting for bright and beautiful colours.

Have fun!

ISBN: 978-1-530906734